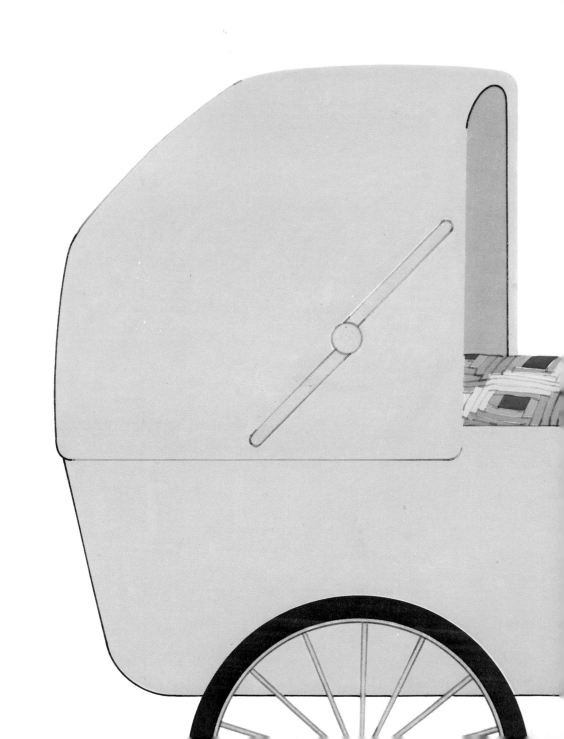

When You Were a Baby

Ann Jonas

Greenwillow Books/New York

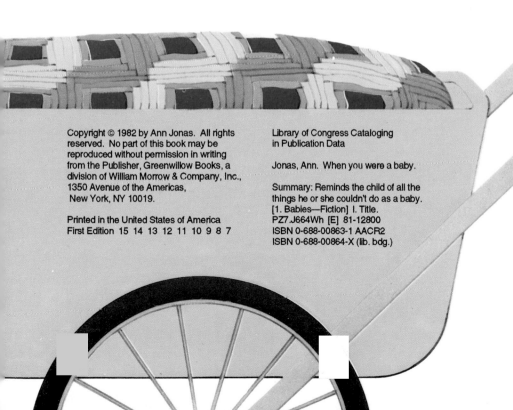

Copyright © 1982 by Ann Jonas. All rights
reserved. No part of this book may be
reproduced without permission in writing
from the Publisher, Greenwillow Books, a
division of William Morrow & Company, Inc.,
1350 Avenue of the Americas,
New York, NY 10019.

Printed in the United States of America
First Edition 15 14 13 12 11 10 9 8 7

Library of Congress Cataloging
in Publication Data

Jonas, Ann. When you were a baby.

Summary: Reminds the child of all the
things he or she couldn't do as a baby.
[1. Babies—Fiction] I. Title.
PZ7.J664Wh [E] 81-12800
ISBN 0-688-00863-1 AACR2
ISBN 0-688-00864-X (lib. bdg.)

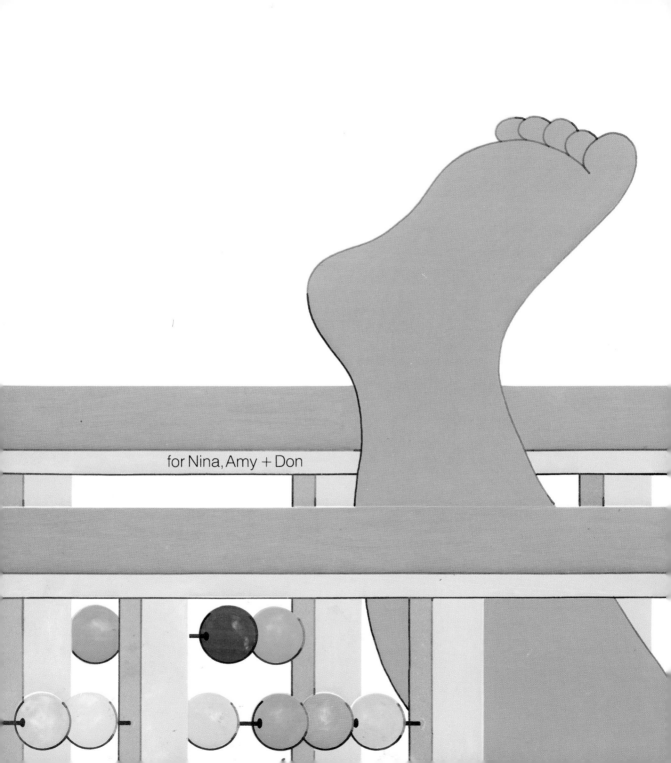

for Nina, Amy + Don

When
you were
a baby,
you couldn't
do very much.

You
couldn't
pile
your
blocks
so high,

or take
your
kitty
for
a ride,

or splash
in puddles
in your
new boots.

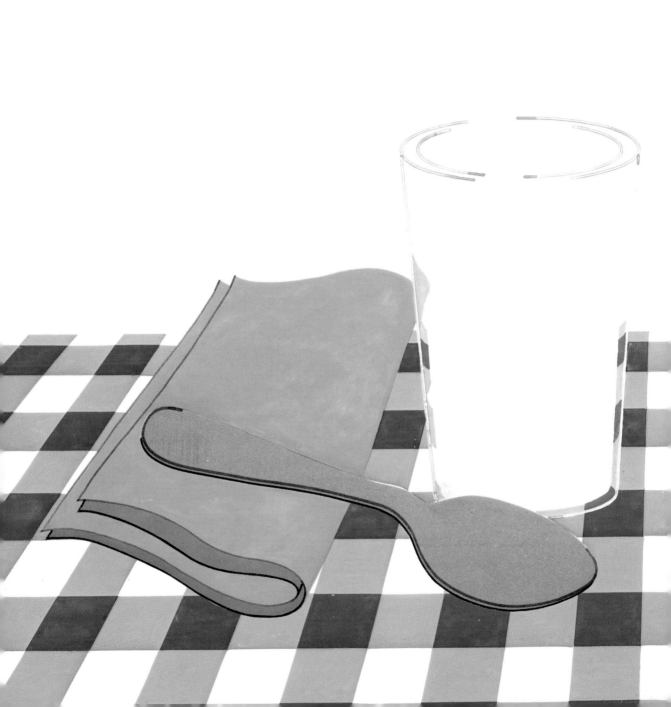

You didn't drink
from a glass
or eat
with a spoon.

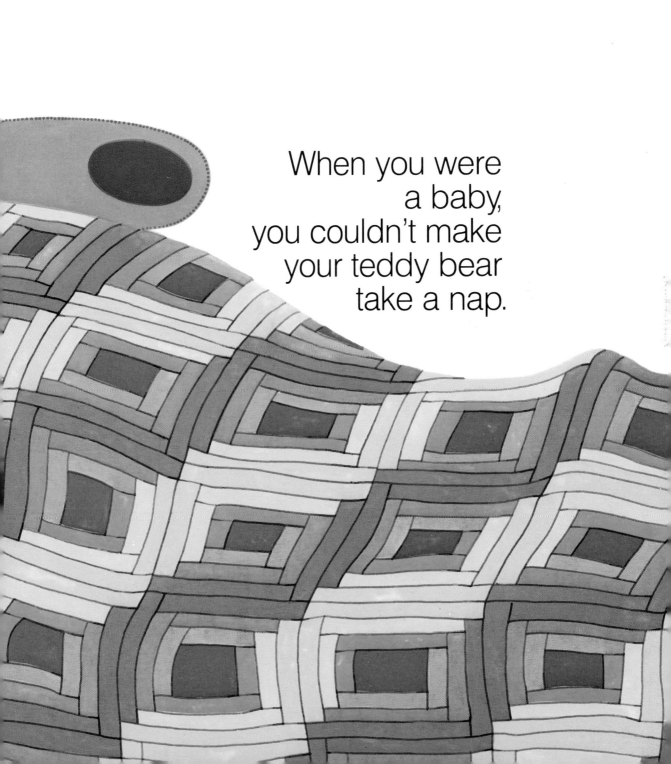

When you were
a baby,
you couldn't make
your teddy bear
take a nap.

You couldn't
roll your ball
across the floor,

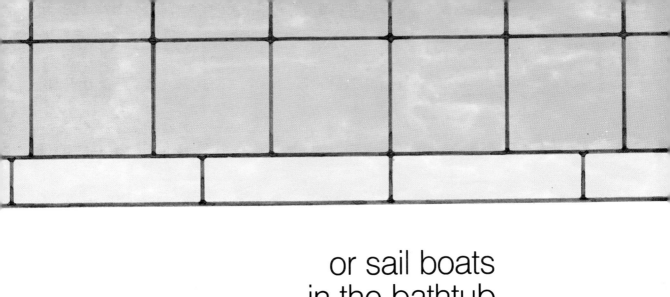

or sail boats
in the bathtub.

When you were a baby,
you couldn't
teach your doll
to sit in a chair,

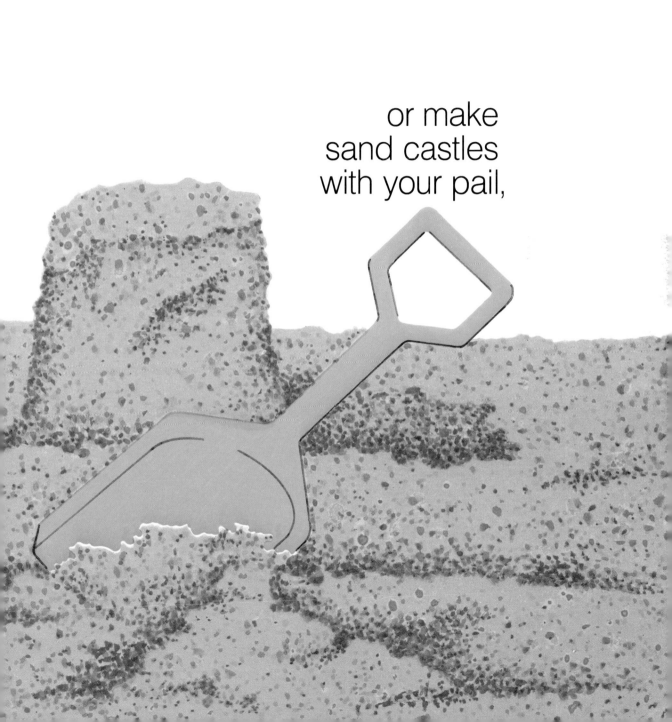

or make
sand castles
with your pail,

or take your dog
for a walk.

But now you can!